On Living Simply

Saint John Chrysostom

On Living Simply

The Golden Voice of
John Chrysostom

Compiled by Robert Van de Weyer

Triumph™ Books
Liguori, Missouri

Published by Triumph™ Books
Liguori, Missouri
An Imprint of Liguori Publications

Library of Congress Cataloging-in-Publication Data

John Chrysostom, Saint, d. 407
    [John Chrysostom]
    On living simply : the golden voice of John Chrysostom / compiled by Robert Van de Weyer. — 1st U.S. ed.
       p.   cm.
    Originally published: John Chrysostom. Evesham, Worcestershire [England] : Arthur James Ltd., 1996.
    ISBN 0-7648-0056-6
    1. Simplicity—Religious aspects—Christianity. 2. Christianity and justice. 3. Christian life. I. Van de Weyer, Robert. II. Title.
BV4647.S48J64 1997
252'.014—dc21   96-39148

Originally published in English by Arthur James Ltd. Publishers under the title *John Chrysostom: The Golden Voice of Protest.*

Text Copyright © 1996 by Robert Van de Weyer
Printed in the United States of America
First U.S. Edition 1997
97 98 99 00 01   5 4 3 2 1

Introduction

When in 312 Emperor Constantine made Christianity the official religion of his scattered empire, the bishops and clergy suddenly found power and wealth accumulating in their hands; after centuries of persecution and poverty, they could now count themselves among the most privileged members of society. Many rejoiced in their new position, building themselves luxurious palaces and villas, and strutting about in sumptuous robes. But a significant minority was aghast, urging the Church to recall the simplicity and the generosity which Christ both preached and practiced. The most eloquent of these opponents was a Syrian called John, trained in the rhetoric of the law courts, whose sermons on the theme of economic and social justice were copied and read throughout the Mediterranean world. He was eventually driven into exile by an empress and a patriarch, who rightly saw him as a threat to the political order. After his death the common people gave him the surname by which he has been known ever since—and which literally means "golden-mouthed."

John Chrysostom was born in about 347 in Antioch, one of the major cities of the Roman Empire. His family were wealthy aristocrats, and throughout his life he exuded the self-assurance which his upbringing gave him.

He learned the art of legal rhetoric under a great pagan orator called Libanius; but in 368 he renounced his career as an advocate, received baptism, and then devoted himself to studying the Scriptures. He felt compelled by the teachings of Christ to give away his wealth, and for a period he went to live as a hermit in a cave. He eventually returned to Antioch where he was ordained a priest. He now dedicated himself to preaching. During the following ten years, he delivered a sermon at least once a week, usually lasting more than two hours. He wrote them out beforehand; afterward scribes copied them, and they were then sent to numerous other church communities to be read. Although he sometimes tackled more theological subjects, he persistently returned to the subject of justice. He argued that rich people should see themselves as stewards of their wealth, lent to them by God to be used for the common good. In the most vehement language he denounced those who live in luxury, without thought for the poor; and his most stinging invective was for those who make conspicuous displays of generosity to the church, buying new chalices and robes for the priest, yet ignoring the beggars at their gates. He saw the Eucharist as a symbol for the political and moral values he proclaimed.

In 389 when the old patriarch of Constantinople died, there was a strong movement among the common people of the city for John to fill the post. The Emperor eventually agreed to invite John, who at first refused, but then—when he realized that he was the people's choice—accepted. He set about his new task with unrelenting energy. He increased the number of hospitals and schools run by the Church, and rooted out corruption among the clergy. He stripped the patriarch's palace of all its lavish ornaments and furniture, and gave the proceeds to the poor. He frequently visited the slums of the city, going about on foot and talking to the people, and often ventured out to the villages and homesteads in the region. He continued to preach week by week, accusing the rich of insulting God himself by their greed.

The people of the city flocked to hear him, and their anger toward their wealthy oppressors became stronger with every sermon they heard. Soon the city authorities began to fear that riots would break out; and Empress Eudoxia—who exemplified all that John loathed—urged her husband to expel him. A large section of the clergy also voiced their anxieties, and were backed by the patriarch of Alexandria, who was jealous of John's fame. A synod of bishops and clergy was convened which brought a number of spurious charges against John; he was found guilty and deposed, with the threat of exile if he continued to preach. The people of the city were outraged, and within a few days John was reinstated to prevent conflict. But two months later John preached a sermon that the empress interpreted—perhaps rightly—as directed against herself; and at her insistence John was abducted while he was celebrating Communion at Easter. He seems to have anticipated his fate, because shortly before his abduction he preached a sermon in which he lamented his imminent exile from the city.

Initially, he was taken to a small town in Armenia. The pope intervened on his behalf; and there was continuing unrest in the city. The bishops decided that John's death was the only means of ensuring peace. So they persuaded the emperor to order John to be taken to a fortress at the eastern end of the Black Sea. He was compelled to travel on foot during the autumn rains, wearing only a few rags. He died on the journey, with the words "Glory to God for everything" on his lips. He was aged sixty.

His sermons have lost little of their power in the intervening centuries. His plain, blunt language, and the simple homely images he used to illustrate his message still compel our attention. This book consists of extracts from the sermons that have survived. I have taken the liberty of abridging some passages, and of paraphrasing others, to make them more accessible to the modern reader. Most of the extracts are on the political and social themes which dominated his sermons. But I have also included some remarkably sensitive pieces on marriage and family life, and on the principles of Christian morality. One suspects that John Chrysostom would be as unpopular today among the privileged members of society as he was in the fourth century—and as popular among the common people.

ROBERT VAN DE WEYER

1

The rich usually imagine that, if they do not physically rob the poor, they are committing no sin. But the sin of the rich consists in not sharing their wealth with the poor. In fact, the rich person who keeps all his wealth for himself is committing a form of robbery. The reason is that in truth all wealth comes from God, and so belongs to everyone equally. The proof of this is all around us. Look at the succulent fruits which the trees and bushes produce. Look at the fertile soil which yields each year such an abundant harvest. Look at the sweet grapes on the vines, which give us wine to drink. The rich may claim that they own many fields in which fruits and grain grow; but it is God who causes seeds to sprout and mature. The duty of the rich is to share the harvest of their fields with all who work in them and with all in need.

2

We do not need to buy air, water, fire, sunshine, and things of this kind. God has given enough of all these blessings for everyone to enjoy them freely. The sun shines equally on the rich and the poor, and they both breathe the same air. Why is it, then, that these necessary things, which sustain life, are created by God for common use, while money is not common? The reason is twofold: to safeguard life and to open the path to virtue. On the one hand if the necessities of life were not common, the rich, with their usual greediness, would take them away from the poor. In fact, since they keep all money for themselves, they would certainly do the same with these necessities. On the other hand if money were common and available to all, there would be no opportunity for generosity on the part of the rich and gratitude on the part of the poor.

Remember how we have been created. All human beings have a common ancestor. Thus all human flesh has the same substance; there is no difference between the flesh of the nobility and that of peasants. When we commit an act of charity, in which we use our excess wealth to help someone with too little, we are acknowledging our unity with others. After all, the rich and the poor have the same flesh, the hunger of the poor should cause pain to the rich; and the pain can only be soothed through assuaging that hunger. Sadly, rich people often speak about charity, expressing their good intentions, but their deeds do not match their words. Good intentions give some cause for hope: they mean that the rich recognize their unity with the poor. Our challenge is to persuade the rich to turn words into actions. Preachers must try to do this; and so also must everyone who has an opportunity to speak to the rich.

4

Commerce in itself is not bad; indeed it is an intrinsic part of God's order. What matters is how we conduct our commerce. The reason why commerce is necessary is that God created human beings with different ambitions and skills. One person is a good carpenter, another a good preacher; one person can make crops grow in the poorest soil, another can heal the most terrible diseases. Thus each person specializes in the work for which God has ordained him; and by selling his skills, or the goods he produces, he can obtain from others the goods which he needs. The problems arise because some people can obtain a far higher price for their work than others, or because some people employ others and do not pay a fair wage. The result is that some become rich and others poor. But in God's eyes one skill is not superior to another; every form of honest labor is equal. So inequalities in what people receive for their labor undermine the divine order.

5

In a family the husband needs the wife to prepare his food; to make, mend, and wash his clothes; to fetch water; and to keep the rooms and furniture in the house clean. The wife needs the husband to till the soil, to build and repair the house, and to earn money to buy the goods they need. God has put into a man's heart the capacity to love his wife, and into a woman's heart the capacity to love her husband. But their mutual dependence makes them love each other out of necessity also. At times love within the heart may not be sufficient to maintain the bond of marriage. But love which comes from material necessity will give that bond the strength it needs to endure times of difficulty. The same is true for society as a whole. God has put into every person's heart the capacity to love his neighbors. But that love is immeasurably strengthened by their dependence on one another's skills.

Share what you have, lest you lose what you have. Spend what you possess on the needs of others in order to keep what you possess. Do not cling to what you own, lest it be taken away from you. Do not hoard your treasures, lest they rot and become worthless. Entrust all your wealth to God, because then it is protected against all who want to steal or destroy it. Do you understand what these injunctions mean? Or do they sound like nonsense to you? To the person without faith, they mean nothing. But to the person with faith, they make perfect sense. Faith tells us that God alone can supply the material things on which we depend. He gives some people more than they need, not that they can enjoy great luxury, but to make them stewards of his bounty on behalf of orphans, the sick, and the crippled. If they are bad stewards, keeping this bounty to themselves, they will become poor in spirit, and their hearts will fill with misery. If they are good stewards, they will become rich in spirit, their hearts filling with joy.

7

The sins of the rich, such as greed and selfishness, are obvious for all to see. The sins of the poor are less conspicuous, yet equally corrosive of the soul. Some poor people are tempted to envy the rich; indeed this is a form of vicarious greed, because the poor person wanting great wealth is in spirit no different from the rich person amassing great wealth. Many poor people are gripped by fear: their hearts are caught in a chain of anxiety, worrying whether they will have food on their plates tomorrow or clothes on their backs. Some poor people are constantly formulating in their minds devious plans to cheat the rich to obtain their wealth; this is no different in spirit from the rich making plans to exploit the poor by paying low wages. The art of being poor is to trust in God for everything, to demand nothing—and to be grateful for all that is given.

8

When a family falls into poverty, it may be compelled to borrow money in order to survive. But if the lender charges interest on the loan, then that family will fall deeper into the pit: not only will they have to repay the loan but also the interest that accumulates on it. The lender may pretend, even to himself, that he is acting kindly; but in fact behind the guise of charity he is acting with extreme malice. He is trading on the calamities of others; he is drawing profit from their distress; he is demanding a material reward for an act of charity, and so turning charity into robbery. He seems to be beckoning the poor family into a safe harbor, but in truth he is taking their ship onto the rocks. The lender may ask: "Why should I lend to others money that is useful to me, and demand no reward for it?" My answer is that you shall receive a reward: in return for the gold you lend on earth, you shall receive gold in heaven at a far greater rate of interest than you could ever imagine.

Imagine a carpenter with the crudest of tools. It takes him many days to make a simple table; and its quality is so low that the price he obtains for it is poor. He has a choice: either he can spend all the money he earns on food and drink or he can set some money aside, even if it means going hungry, in order to buy better tools. If he does the latter, then he will soon be making good tables much more quickly, and so his earnings will quickly rise. This choice is analogous to a spiritual choice that each of us must make. Either we can spend for our own pleasure all the wealth we possess or we can set aside part of our wealth to give to others. If we do the latter, then we may sacrifice a few immediate, earthly pleasures; but the joy we earn for ourselves in heaven far, far surpasses the pleasure we have lost on earth. Every act of charity on earth is an investment in heaven.

10

We who are disciples of Christ claim that our purpose on earth is to lay up treasures in heaven. But our actions often belie our words. Many Christians build for themselves fine houses, lay out splendid gardens, construct bathhouses, and buy fields. It is small wonder, then, that many pagans refuse to believe what we say. "If their eyes are set on mansions in heaven," they ask, "why are they building mansions on earth? If they put their words into practice, they would give away their riches and live in simple huts." So these pagans conclude that we do not sincerely believe in the religion we profess; and as a result they refuse to take this religion seriously. You may say that the words of Christ on these matters are too hard for you to follow; and that while your spirit is willing, your flesh is weak. My answer is that the judgment of the pagans about you is more accurate than your judgment of yourself. When the pagans accuse us of hypocrisy, many of us should plead guilty.

11

Some people see the houses in which they live as their kingdom; and although in their minds they know that death will one day force them to leave, in their hearts they feel they will stay forever. They take pride in the size of their houses and the fine materials with which they are built. They take pleasure in decorating their houses with bright colors, and in obtaining the best and most solid furniture to fill the rooms. They imagine that they can find peace and security by owning a house whose walls and roof will last for many generations. We, by contrast, know that we are only temporary guests on earth. We recognize that the houses in which we live serve only as hostels on the road to eternal life. We do not seek peace or security from the material walls around us or the roof above our heads. Rather, we want to surround ourselves with a wall of divine grace; and we look upward to heaven as our roof. And the furniture of our lives should be good works, performed in a spirit of love.

12

When we live according to the moral principles of our faith, those around us may respond in three possible ways. First, they may be so impressed by the example of our goodness, and so envious of the joy which it brings, that they want to join us and become like us. That is the response which we most earnestly desire. Second, they may be indifferent to us, because they are so bound up with their own selfish cares and concerns; although their eyes may perceive our way of life, their hearts are blind, so we are unable to stir them. Third, they may react against us, feeling threatened by our example and even angry with us; thus they will cling even more firmly to their material possessions and selfish ambitions, and slander us at every opportunity. Naturally, we dread this third type of reaction, because we want to live in peace with our neighbors, regardless of their personal beliefs and values. But if no one reacts to us in this way, we must wonder whether we are truly fulfilling the commandments of Christ.

13

Do you feel upset when you drop a plate or a pot, and it smashes into tiny pieces on the ground? Do you feel anxious when a strong wind is blowing, and you can hear the tiles on your roof coming loose? Do you feel worried about the crops in your field when it rains so hard that the ground is flooded? Do you feel frightened at night when you hear a door click or squeak, wondering if robbers have come to steal your goods? To feel those things is quite normal. Yet the challenge of our faith is that we become so indifferent to material possessions that nothing of this kind can concern us. Of course while we remain on this earth, we must have plates on which to serve our food, roofs above our heads to keep us dry, crops growing in the fields to feed us, and some basic pieces of furniture in our homes. But if we work hard day by day to the best of our abilities, we can be sure that God will provide what we need. And if something is broken, lost, or stolen, God will decide if and when to replace it.

14

One person has the skill to hammer brass into the most exquisite shapes and to engrave elaborate patterns on to it. Another has the skill to make furniture, joining together different pieces of wood so firmly that no one can break them apart. A third person can spin the finest yarn, while a fourth weaves it into cloth. A fifth craftsperson can lay stones one on top of the other to build walls, while a sixth puts a roof on top of the walls to make a house. Indeed there are so many different skills, each one requiring many years to attain, that it would be impossible to list them all. So what is the skill that rich people should acquire? They do not need to fashion brass or wood, or to build houses. Rather, they must learn how to use their wealth well, to the good of all the people around them. The ordinary craftsperson may think that that is an easy skill to learn. On the contrary, it is the hardest skill of all. It requires both great wisdom and great moral strength. Look at how many rich people fail to acquire it, and how few practice it to perfection.

When a tailor makes and sells a garment, only one service is performed, that of putting clothes on a body. The same is true of a cobbler making and selling a pair of shoes; the only service in this case is to put shoes on the feet. But when a person makes a gift to another person, of money or some object, a double service is performed. First, the receiver derives a material benefit from the gift. Second, the giver derives a spiritual benefit, because this act of generosity will have brought a blessing to his soul. And there can even be a third service: if the receiver is filled with humble gratitude that will be a blessing to that person's soul. Imagine a society in which no one sold anything, but everyone shared freely their skills and wealth. Then every action in that society would bring not only material benefits, but spiritual benefits also. Such societies already exist in miniature: families operate in this way. How wonderful it would be if villages and towns could become like large families. Then heaven would come down to earth.

The amount we give is not judged by the largeness of the gifts but the largeness of our hearts. The poor woman who shares her meager pot of stew with another poor woman is far more to be praised than the rich man who throws a few gold coins into a collection at church. But although most Christians acknowledge the truth of this, their words and actions convey a different message. When a rich man makes a large gift to the church, he is heartily thanked; and although he will not feel the lack of that money himself, he is praised for his generosity. When a poor man makes a small gift, nothing is said; even though that gift may cause him to go hungry, no one praises him or thanks him. It would be better to praise no one than to confine our praise to the rich. Better still, we should take trouble to observe every true act of generosity, whether by the rich or the poor, and then offer our praise. Indeed let us be as generous with our praise as people are generous with their money.

Consider how an ear of corn is produced. Most of us would point to the labor of the farmer in tilling the soil, sowing the seed, and harvesting the grain. But it is not as simple as that. The farmer needs the blacksmith to make the spade, ploughshare, sickle, and axe. He needs the carpenter to make a frame for the plough and to make a yoke for the horse. He needs the leather worker to make the harness. He needs the builder to make a stable for the horse, and a barn to store the hay and grain. He needs a baker to turn the grain into bread, otherwise his labors are worthless. And he needs the forest worker to provide wood for the carpenter to saw, and wood for the baker to heat the oven. So just to produce corn many different people are needed. Since we depend on one another for our very survival, why do we ever try to exploit and cheat one another? Nothing could be more stupid and irrational than to try and get the better of someone else; people who cheat and exploit others are cheating and exploiting themselves.

18

You tell me that you need money. You say that money is necessary to enable you to buy the things you need. I do not disagree with you. I, too, require money in order to survive. But I wish that I did not need money. Or rather I wish that none of us needed money. God tells us to trust him to provide for all our needs. I wish we could trust other people also to provide what we need. Indeed as a preacher I am forced to do this. I proclaim the truth of God; and I depend entirely on the gifts of those who hear me—gifts which usually come in the form of money. Others among you make things. If all of you gave to others freely what you have made, money would become unnecessary. If each of you took trouble to observe the needs of others, and then according to your abilities freely met those needs, none of us would need money. And no one would go hungry or cold; all would have sufficient.

19

The skill which the rich need to use their wealth well is the highest of all arts. Its workshop is built not on earth but in heaven, because those who are rich must communicate directly with God to acquire and practice this art. Its tools are not made of iron or brass, but of good will, because the rich will only use their wealth well if they want to do so. Indeed good will is itself the skill. When a rich person sincerely wants to help the poor, God will quickly show the best way. Thus while a person training to be a carpenter must learn how to control a hammer and saw and chisel, the rich person training to serve the poor must learn how to control the mind and heart and soul. He must learn always to think good thoughts, expunging all selfish thoughts. He must learn how to feel compassion, expunging all malice and contempt. He must learn how to desire only to obey the will of God. That is why I say the skill of being a rich disciple of Christ is the highest of all arts; and the one who possesses it is truly a saint.

I often speak of the rich and the poor. I would rather not have to speak in these terms. If everyone acted according to the teachings of Christ, there would be no rich and poor; all would be equal. This is because the rich would continue giving away their wealth until everyone had the same. Since only a minority have truly embraced the teachings of Christ, this is not going to happen. But we can make a start; and the place to start is the Church. Let the rich give liberally to their church congregations. Then let each congregation use this bounty to support widows and orphans, the sick and the crippled. And let those whom God has called to perpetual virginity be the primary means through which this bounty is channeled. Hospitals and schools can be built where those in need can come, and where those called to celibacy can serve them. The rich would take no pride in their gifts, because those receiving the gifts would not know their names; their gratitude could be directed only to the Church. So let your particular church become in this way a reflection on earth of the glory of heaven.

All of us are liable to complain of our work. We grumble at the hardness of our work, at its monotony and dullness, at the lack of time to rest and relax. We moan about how weary we feel. And we wish that we were wealthy enough to be free of work. But just imagine what perpetual leisure actually means. In your mind let me give you a large house in which to live, filled with comfortable furniture. In this house you only need to nod at a servant, and you will be brought dish upon dish of the most delicious food. Outside there is a garden filled with trees and shrubs, which bear sweet-smelling flowers. For a few hours, for a few days perhaps, you would enjoy being in such a place. But soon you would feel bored and restless. Your bones would become still for lack of exercise. Your stomach would swell with all that food. Your head would ache for lack of anything to stimulate the mind. Your mansion in which work was impossible would seem like a prison. God has designed us to labor for our bread; only in toil can our minds and bodies find contentment.

Those who love money are fierce in the pursuit of it, like wild animals pursuing their prey. They do not allow the ties of friendship to restrain them; they betray, cheat, or exploit their closest friends when there is gold and silver to be gained. Nor do they let the chains of conscience inhibit them; they learn to make their consciences as numb as fingers on a cold day. Even members of their own families may be used in their quest for wealth. Their eyes become blind to the suffering they cause, and their ears deaf to the cries of those whose lives are ruined by them. They imagine themselves to be free, pursuing their own interests without constraint. Yet in truth they are slaves to their own greed; and this greed only brings them misery. So they bring a double misery into the world, to those they exploit and to themselves. Worst of all, they are even grateful for their own greed; they give thanks that this desire for money motivates their actions and gives purpose to their lives. While they feel this gratitude, they can never escape.

We may observe people worshiping statues, and we accuse them of idolatry. We say that these lumps of wood, clay, or metal are lifeless, and so possess no divine qualities. Indeed we find the idea of worshiping statues so bizarre that we even laugh with contempt at those who do it. Yet far more dangerous than statues that are visible are the numerous idols which are invisible. Power is such an idol. Some people who possess powerful personalities desire power for themselves, and in this way make it their idol. Others like to be under the sway of a powerful personality, who makes decisions on their behalf, and in this way releases them from the task of making moral choices for themselves; thus they make the powerful person their idol. Fame is another invisible idol. Some people with the gift of speech love to bask in the warmth of adulation, and so make the admiration of others their idol. Those others find perverse pleasure in treating the gifted speaker as a god, whose every word must be treated as infallible. What I am saying is that the most dangerous idols are not outward objects made of wood and clay, but reside inside the human heart.

have observed that there are two types of rich people. The first enjoys spreading his wealth: he loves to live in a fine house, surrounded by beautiful furniture, and to eat the most expensive food. The second enjoys keeping his wealth: he would rather live in a hovel, as long as he possessed a chest full of gold and silver coins; and his greatest pleasure is to sit at a table, counting out his money. Which type of rich person can most easily be redeemed? Without doubt it is the first. The rich man who likes spending his money usually enjoys welcoming others into his home, so they can admire his wealth; and he takes pride in welcoming them to his table, to enjoy a sumptuous banquet. That openness to others can, with effort, be transformed into a genuine desire to share his wealth with others. But the miser who hoards his money has a heart that is closed and dark; and it is almost impossible to pry open the door of his heart in order to let the light enter. If a rich man invites me to a banquet, I may accept, hoping to convert him. But the miser never invites anyone into his home or his heart.

Nothing is more frigid than a Christian who is indifferent to the salvation of others. Indeed I wonder if such a person can be a true Christian. To become a disciple of Christ is to obey his law of love; and obedience to the law brings joy beyond measure and description. Love means to want the best for others, sharing with them the joy of love. So the Christian feels compelled to speak to others about the law of love, and the joy of obeying this law. Of course, many people are shy about speaking to others; in their case actions motivated by love will be a most eloquent testimony. But those who are not shy will surely want to express their joy at every opportunity. There is no need to use fine words or elegant phrases; even the most uneducated people can convey joyful love by the spirit which accompanies their words. Even slaves have been known to convert their masters and mistresses by the sincerity of their speech.

Slavery is an abomination. It is quite wrong that one person should buy another, and that such a purchase has the protection of the law. A person does not even possess his own life; so how can he possess another person's life? Yet this does not mean that slaves should be disobedient to their masters, nor that they should try to escape their condition. To be a slave, to be in the legal possession of another human being, does not in any way impede spiritual salvation. On the contrary, by performing his duties with a humble spirit, a slave may advance the progress of his soul. Even if the tasks he performs are useless in themselves, the attitude with which he undertakes those tasks is profoundly important. Similarly, masters need not necessarily feel compelled to release their slaves. In some cases, where the slave has sufficient wisdom and strength to make his way in the world, this may be right. But in other cases, where the slave would be plunged into poverty and destitution, it is better that the master keeps the slave and looks after him well.

War is an abomination. It is quite wrong that one nation or tribe should attack another in pursuit of land, power, or wealth. It is doubly wrong that the victors should proclaim the glory of their battles, while their victims lie maimed and dying. The glory of war is illusory; war brings only misery. Yet this does not mean that military service is a dishonorable profession, nor that carrying arms impedes salvation. Every emperor, king, and prince must have soldiers to protect his realm from attack, and his people from robbery and murder. An army is necessary to keep peace with other nations, and to keep peace within a nation. What, then, if the king orders his army to perform an evil act, such as invading a neighboring nation? Should the Christian soldier disobey his orders, even at the risk of being executed for his disobedience? In such a situation he must weigh one evil against another: the evil of participating in the invasion, against the evil of leaving his family without material support. None of us can presume to judge the soldier's decision, but rather we must pray that the Spirit guides his conscience.

God has created all people spiritually equal. Every person has the same propensity for good and evil. Every person has the same choice, as to whether to obey God or to defy him. Yet in other ways, we are very unequal. Some people are highly intelligent, while others have feeble intellects. Some people are physically strong and healthy, while others are weak and prone to illness. Some people are handsome and attractive, while others are plain. Those who are gifted in some way should not despise those less gifted. On the contrary, God has distributed gifts and blessings in such a way that every person has a particular place and purpose within a society—and thus everyone is equally necessary for a society to function well. So do not resent the fact that someone is more intelligent or stronger than you are. Instead give thanks for their intelligence and strength, from which you benefit. And then ask yourself: "What is my gift, and thence what is my place in society?" When you have answered this question, and you act according to your answer, all contempt and all resentment will melt away.

Do I possess the house in which I live? No, it is only on loan to me from God while I remain in that place. Do I possess the clothes I wear? No, they are on loan to me until they wear out, or until I give them away to someone in greater need. Do I possess this body that you see before you? No, it was lent to me by God when I was born, and he will take it back when I die. Do I possess the mind that is composing the words that I speak? No, that too was lent by God at my birth and will go when I die. So do I possess anything? Yes, I possess the virtues which during my life have grown and flourished within my soul. Inasmuch as I have grown in love, I possess love. Inasmuch as I have grown in faith, I possess faith. Inasmuch as I have grown in gentleness, I possess gentleness. These things are immortal; they are divine gifts which God will not take away, because he wants heaven itself to be filled with virtue. And, of course, I possess my soul, in which these virtues have their roots.

30

When you are generous to another person, you are not bestowing a gift, but repaying a debt. Everything you possess materially comes from God, who created all things. And every spiritual and moral virtue you possess is through divine grace. Thus you owe everything to God. More than that, God has given you his Son, to show you how to live: how to use your material possessions, and how to grow in moral and spiritual virtue. We may say that your material and spiritual possession cost God nothing; God created the universe in order to express his own glory. But the gift of his Son was supremely costly, because his Son suffered and died for our sakes. The agony of Christ on the cross is the measure of how much God loves us. For this reason we should take none of our gifts—material or spiritual—for granted; day by day we should give thanks to God for what he has bestowed on us. Once this spirit of gratitude infuses us, we shall see generosity for what it is. When we help someone in need, we shall be saved from any temptation to take pride in our actions. On the contrary, we will regard our act as no more than a small token of appreciation for all that we have received—or, more precisely, the repayment of a tiny fraction of God's blessings.

Go outside into a field. Ask yourself: "To whom does this field belong?" And you will reply to yourself: "It belongs to me" or "It belongs to so-and-so." Then ask yourself: "To whom has this field belonged in the past?" If you know the history of that field, a list of names will appear in your mind. Then you will realize how little ownership means. That field has seen countless generations of people claiming ownership of it. Countless generations of feet have trod on it, have plowed its soil, and have sown and harvested grain. If the field were sentient, do you think it would feel owned by the person who claims ownership? Of course not. The field would feel that it owned itself and was welcoming the person who claimed ownership merely as a visitor. That is the way we should always think of ourselves on this earth: we are merely visitors, here for a short span to learn virtue; then after that span we shall continue our journey toward the kingdom that lasts forever.

A man decides to build a house. He digs down into the earth until he reaches solid rock, and then lays the foundations. He collects great lumps of stone, hews them into regular shapes, and puts them one on top of the other to make walls. He goes into the forest to chop down trees, which he saws into rafters for the roof. He digs out clay, and bakes it into tiles to put on the roof. At last his work is complete. He stands back and admires his achievement. "Nothing can destroy such a strong building," he says to himself; "my house will last forever." Certainly such a man is skilled with his hands; but he is totally unskilled with his soul. Even if his house were to last forever, it is utterly irrelevant to him. He may be struck down by an accident or a disease within a few days. He may survive his full span, but as the breath leaves his body, his house will count for nothing. He might just as well have built himself a shelter from sticks and mud and used the time saved to concentrate on the salvation of his own soul.

There are many disciples of Christ who can justly claim that they are indifferent to material possessions. They happily live in simple huts, wear rough woolen clothes, eat frugally, and give away the bulk of their fortunes. These same people can justly claim that they are indifferent to worldly power. They happily work in the most humble capacities, performing menial tasks, with no desire for high rank. But there may still be one earthly attribute to which they cling: reputation. They may wish to be regarded by others as virtuous. They may want to be admired for their charity, their honesty, their integrity, their self-denial. They may not actually draw people's attention to these qualities, but they are pleased to know that others respect them. Thus when someone falsely accuses them of some wrongdoing, they react with furious indignation. They protect their reputation with the same ferocity as the rich people protect their gold. Giving up material possessions and worldly power is easy compared with giving up reputation. To be falsely accused and yet to remain spiritually serene is the ultimate test of faith.

Think of the rich person lying on a soft couch munching succulent fruit and sweetmeats, the lights in his house burning bright. It begins to rain, and a few drops come through the ceiling. He orders his slaves to go out onto the roof and mend the leak at once, so he can relax undisturbed. Can this rich person pray? Of course not. His mind is so anxious to maintain and enhance his wealth, and he becomes so worried at the smallest blemish or fault in his material assets that his soul has no space for God's Spirit. Think now of the poor man lying in the gutter outside the rich man's house, competing with dogs for the scraps of food which the rich man has thrown out. It begins to rain, and his clothes become drenched; he has no shelter, so he must shiver with cold. Can this poor man pray? Hardly. His mind is so preoccupied with his own bodily survival, and even a shower of rain poses a further threat to his well-being, that his soul has no space for God's Spirit. The most precious fruit of material justice is prayer.

We have a paradox. On the one hand we know that material justice can only be achieved if the hearts of the rich are changed, so that they freely share their wealth with the poor. On the other hand the hearts of the rich are so preoccupied with maintaining and enhancing their wealth that they have neither time nor space to consider matters of religion and morality. So how can we break this paradox? In the life of every rich man, there are moments when the light of truth penetrates his heart, when he realizes that his wealth does not bring happiness, but only brings misery. These moments may be rare and fleeting. But when they occur we, who have been blessed by God with knowledge of the truth, must be ready to speak to the rich man and persuade him to change his life in response to that light. This is the reason why our contact with the rich must be as close as our contact with the poor. We must make friends with the rich and win their trust, so we can be ready to seize every spiritual opportunity as it occurs.

There are two sorts of arts. There are those arts necessary for survival: these are the arts concerned with growing crops, making clothes, and building houses. Without food, clothing, and shelter we should die; so the arts associated with producing these things are noble and fine. Then there are arts whose purpose is to provide luxuries, such as confectionery, embroidery, sculpture, and so on. I do not regard these latter arts as superfluous. For example, it is right that we should adorn our churches with embroidered cloth and sculptured stone. It is right also that we should celebrate our festivals with delicious sweetmeats. And it is good that even the humblest of families should enjoy a few luxuries, to bring pleasure to their lives. Yet when luxuries become normal we should be ashamed. When the decoration that we lavish on the house of God is also lavished on the houses of human beings, the pleasure which they afford turns to dust—and the sight of such private luxury is morally obscene. The test of a good society is that the great majority are engaged in the basic arts, and only a few in the arts of luxury. When large numbers are engaged in producing luxuries for the rich, that society has become corrupt.

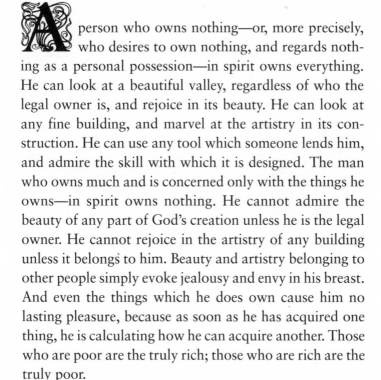

A person who owns nothing—or, more precisely, who desires to own nothing, and regards nothing as a personal possession—in spirit owns everything. He can look at a beautiful valley, regardless of who the legal owner is, and rejoice in its beauty. He can look at any fine building, and marvel at the artistry in its construction. He can use any tool which someone lends him, and admire the skill with which it is designed. The man who owns much and is concerned only with the things he owns—in spirit owns nothing. He cannot admire the beauty of any part of God's creation unless he is the legal owner. He cannot rejoice in the artistry of any building unless it belongs to him. Beauty and artistry belonging to other people simply evoke jealousy and envy in his breast. And even the things which he does own cause him no lasting pleasure, because as soon as he has acquired one thing, he is calculating how he can acquire another. Those who are poor are the truly rich; those who are rich are the truly poor.

The art of being poor in spirit is to distinguish between use and ownership. A person who owns something—or regards himself as owner—believes he has the sole right to determine how that thing is used. He may use it himself or authorize another person to use it. But this sense of ownership is a terrible snare, because it prevents a person's soul from marching onward to God. The person who wishes to move toward God must free himself from all sense of ownership. He must regard all things as loans from God, even the things which he himself owns. A loan is to be used for a period, and then paid back. This is precisely how we should regard our houses and fields, clothes and furniture; they are loans which God grants us for our short span on earth, to be repaid at the moment of death. To be poor in spirit does not mean to be destitute, lacking in even the basic comforts and necessities. It means to regard nothing as your own, and everything you have as a temporary loan.

There are some who are rich in material wealth. Others are rich in power. People rich in power seem to carry authority with them, like a wealthy person may carry a bag of gold. In any and every situation people look to them for leadership, asking them to make decisions. And while most people are nervous about making decisions, anxious about being wrong or being criticized by others, the person rich in power seems to make decisions easily. Power, like wealth, can be used for good purposes or bad. The powerful person can manipulate people to personal advantage, exploiting them in order to gain some privilege. Most dangerous of all is when a powerful person enjoys exercising power for its own sake, taking pleasure in seeing people bend to his will. Equally a powerful person may guide and direct people onto the path of righteousness. He may make decisions which benefit others, materially and spiritually, without thought for himself. The powerful person who puts the needs of others before himself is a true hero of our faith.

Look at those who rule your city or your nation. Some seem to have no qualities which mark them out for such a task; they hold a position of power through an accident of birth, or through ingratiating themselves with their superiors. Some have natural authority, so that they inspire confidence and respect in others. Some possess natural wisdom, so they handle easily the complex affairs of state. But whether or not they have natural gifts, there is another type of gift which surpasses all others: the gift of knowing right from wrong, and the courage to choose what is right. This moral gift is not something which is given at birth, and which some people possess and others do not. The potential of moral discernment is like a seed sown in every human heart; and this seed grows only if it is nurtured through reflection, education, prayer, and practice. It would be better that our leaders were poor in natural gifts, but rich in this moral gift, than that they exuded authority and wisdom, but used these natural gifts for their own ends.

41

s every ruler elected by God to the throne he occupies? Is every emperor, king, and prince chosen by rule? If so, is every law and decree promulgated by a ruler to be regarded as good, and thus to be obeyed without question? The answer to all these questions is, no. God has ordained that every society should have rulers, whose task it is to maintain order, so that people may live in peace. God allows rulers to employ soldiers, whose task it is to capture and imprison those who violate social order. Thus God will bless and guide any ruler and any soldier who acts according to these principles. But many rulers abuse their authority by amassing huge wealth for themselves at the expense of their people, by unjustly punishing those who dare to speak against their evil, and by making unjust wars against neighbors. Such rulers have not been elected by God, but rather have usurped the position which a righteous ruler should occupy. And if their laws are wrong, we should not obey them. The supreme authority in all matters is not the law of the land, but the law of God; and if one conflicts with the other, we must obey God's law.

There are three types of government. The first is where one person, or a group of persons, pass laws and issue decrees which everyone must obey. The second is where every person is his own master, acting as he or she thinks fit. The third is where God is acknowledged as ruler, and all people seek to follow his way of love. This third type of government is the ideal to which we should aspire, and for which we should pray. And if every person were truly seeking to follow God's way of love, then we could also have the second type of government. We would know that if people were free to make their own decisions on all matters, these decisions would conform to God's laws, so there would be perfect harmony. However no society has ever existed in which every member fully and consistently tries to obey God; there are always people motivated by greed and self-interest. For this reason there need to be individuals or small groups who pass laws and issue decrees which can be enforced. The existence of the first type of government is a tacit admission of human sin and frailty. The challenge is to ensure that these lawmakers act on behalf of the people as a whole and not just for their own benefit.

43

Should we look to kings and princes to put right the inequalities between rich and poor? Should we require soldiers to come and seize the rich person's gold and distribute it among his destitute neighbors? Should we beg the emperor to impose a tax on the rich so great that it reduces them to the level of the poor and then to share the proceeds of that tax among everyone? Equality imposed by force would achieve nothing, and do much harm. Those who combined both cruel hearts and sharp minds would soon find ways of making themselves rich again. Worse still, the rich whose gold was taken away would feel bitter and resentful; while the poor who received the gold from the hands of soldiers would feel no gratitude, because no generosity would have prompted the gift. Far from bringing moral benefit to society, it would actually do moral harm. Material justice cannot be accomplished by compulsion, a change of heart will not follow. The only way to achieve true justice is to change people's hearts first—and then they will joyfully share their wealth.

44

How should the Church be governed? Should the patriarchs act like emperors, issuing decrees which all believers must obey? Should bishops see themselves as local governors, demanding unquestioning submission of the people? Should the clergy be a kind of spiritual army, enforcing the will of the patriarchs and bishops, and meting out punishment on sinners? The first consideration for the Church is not how to punish sins, but how to prevent sins from being committed. And when a sin has been committed, the task of the Church is to encourage the sinner to confess the sin and make amends—so that no punishment is required. This is a quite different attitude to wrongdoing from that which the state adopts, and so requires a quite different style of government. Moreover, each individual is answerable not to be a priest, bishop, or patriarch, but to God. So the primary authority of those within the Church is not to issue decrees, but to stir the souls and enliven the consciences of believers, so that by their own volition they will obey the laws of God. In short those in authority within the Church should see themselves not as rulers, but as preachers and pastors.

Who is fit to be a leader in the Church? What gifts and qualities should we look for in those who take charge of our spiritual affairs? Should we assess potential leaders by their abilities, such as the ability to preach well, to find the right words to say to the sick and the dying, to interpret with expertise the words of Scripture, and so on? Certainly all these things are important; and without some natural capacities of this kind, a person clearly is not called to be a spiritual leader. But these abilities count for nothing—indeed they are likely to do harm—unless they are firmly based on spiritual and moral qualities. Imagine a person with exceptional rhetorical skills who could inspire any congregation to share his vision. If that vision were rooted in an evil heart, such a person could do terrible damage to the congregation, turning their hearts toward evil also. Imagine a person of great intellectual ability, who twisted the words of Scripture to suit his own wicked purposes. That person could make a congregation believe that good was evil, and evil good. Imagine a person whose voice could bring comfort to every kind of distress, but who was the agent of the devil, not of God, when he visited the dying. Even to mention that such a person may exist is to induce fear in the hearts of every believer.

The way to judge whether a person is called by God to be a Church leader is to look first at his moral qualities. Is he generous to those in need? Is he gentle toward those who are weaker than himself? Is he patient toward those less intelligent than himself? Is he a loyal and faithful friend? Of course, there are many people who are generous, gentle, patient, and loyal, and yet who are not called to be leaders. Second, look at his spiritual qualities. Does he pray regularly and diligently? Does he read the Scriptures with care? Does he sincerely try to hear God's will and obey it? Of course, there are many people who truly love God, and yet are not called to be leaders. There is, however, one quality—or rather a combination of two qualities— which marks out the true Church leader. Is he humble about his own abilities, and at the same time can he discern the abilities of others? The most basic task of the Church leader is to discern the spiritual gifts of all those under his authority, and to encourage those gifts to be used to the full for the benefit of all. Only a person who can discern the gifts of others and can humbly rejoice at the flowering of those gifts is fit to lead the Church.

In the relationship of a pastor with his flock, it is not sufficient for the pastor to express his love for them; he must acknowledge their love for him. There is a kind of pride in the pastor who shows great warmth and generosity to those in his charge, and yet is blind to the warmth and generosity which they show in return. It is as if he is claiming a monopoly of love. But when a pastor expresses gratitude for the love which they have showered upon him, he is affirming their virtue, and thus encouraging them in their Christian journey. The same is true in all personal relationships. The person who just expresses love for his friends but fails to acknowledge their love for him is not a true friend. Loving friendship requires both parties to love each other, and each party to affirm the other's love. Jesus, as both a pastor and a friend, not only poured out love but also made himself dependent on others. He possessed nothing, so for his very survival he had to rely on the kindness of his friends and disciples. And in his gratitude for all he received, he affirmed them as true friends and true disciples.

The greatest test of a friendship is whether one person can reprove the other. All of us commit sins from time to time; and all of us try to blind ourselves to our sins, making excuses for ourselves, or pretending the sin did not even occur. At such times we need friends to open our eyes to the reality of our sins. Put yourself now in the position of the friend. Are you willing to open that person's eyes? Are you willing to expose the excuses as false? Are you prepared to risk that person's wrath, as wounded pride rises up in anger? Or do you prefer to blind yourself to your friend's faults, and so join a conspiracy of blindness? In choosing our friends, we should embrace those who are willing to be honest with us, and those prepared if necessary to endure our anger. Without such honesty the friendship has no depth, and is useless. Yet when it is your duty to express criticism to a friend, beware of destroying that friend's self-respect. Always soften your reproof with words of affirmation, in which you acknowledge their virtue. And ensure that your own motives are good: that love, not jealousy or anger, is the true wellspring of your words.

In every local church congregation we appoint stewards. The stewards have charge of the material possessions of the Christian community. The money which people give is held by the stewards, who dispense it to those in need. The stewards own nothing themselves; nor do they have any independent power. The money they hold is the property of the community; in dispensing that money they must conform to the principles laid down by the community; and in enacting those policies they are answerable to the community. If a steward fails to discharge his duties to the satisfaction of the community, the community may dismiss him and appoint someone else in his place. All this is well understood by every member of a congregation. In the same way each one of us is the steward of the gifts which God has bestowed, both our material wealth and our natural abilities. We do not own those gifts; they belong to God. They are to be used according to the principles which God has laid down. And each one of us is answerable to God as to whether those principles have been followed. If we fail to use our gifts rightly, he may take them away from us; but more likely he will call us to account after death.

I have been given the power of speech. There is no intrinsic merit in this; it is not something for which I should be especially admired or respected. To possess this gift, like any other natural ability, is a blessing bestowed by God; admiration and respect should be directed toward him. The challenge facing me is how I use this gift. Do I develop it through seeking the guidance of accomplished speakers and through practice? More importantly, do I use it in the service of God or of myself? Of course I may also claim to use it in God's service, and even congratulate myself on the excellent sermons I preach. But how easily pride infects the use of this gift. When I hold the attention of a congregation, when each person is concentrating on my every word, when my eloquence stirs every heart that hears me, how easily my head begins to swell. Instead of simply being a mouthpiece of God, I begin to imagine myself divine. The gift of speech, which is truly a blessing, can so easily become a curse, poisoning the soul that possesses it.

People are easily impressed by miracles of healing, in which sick people are made well. But we can see in all our church communities a much greater kind of miracle: ordinary peasants and artisans become great preachers and teachers of the Gospel. There are few educated and well-spoken people in our midst, but the majority in our congregations—like the majority in society as a whole—have received no formal education. Yet inspired by the Holy Spirit some become great philosophers of truth. They are able to hear the words of Christ, to understand the profound import of those words, and then to apply the words to the needs and problems of the people around them. In ancient times it was thought that a person needed to study for many years in a philosophical academy in order to comprehend truth. But even today people are acquiring philosophical expertise with not even a day of training. Is not this a miracle? Is it not a visible sign of the power of the Holy Spirit? Does it not assure us that salvation is for all people, regardless of wealth or rank, education or status? Does it not affirm that Christ's Gospel is for fools—who in the power of the Spirit become wise?

Only a fool would attempt to change the world with a simple message of love and peace. So we can conclude that Jesus was a fool. Only fools would agree to follow such a man, and then continue his mission even after he had been killed. So we can conclude that the apostles were fools. Only fools would take seriously the message which a bunch of fools were preaching, and accept that message. So we can conclude that all of us are fools. All this is hardly surprising. God did not choose a wise philosopher to proclaim the Gospel, but a humble carpenter. And for his apostles he chose fishermen and tax collectors. Can we claim to be any better? Of course not. Even those among us who have been educated know that in relation to the Gospel our education is worthless. So let all happily admit we are fools. Then we will happily commit ourselves to trying to change the world. Yet weren't those apostles cowardly and timid? Aren't we equally afraid of trying to persuade strangers to change their lives? Doesn't the crucifixion of Christ give us ample reason to be frightened? Yes; but his Resurrection gives us superhuman courage.

ook at the trees of the forest. See how sturdy and beautiful they are, how tall they grow, and how smooth is their bark. Yet when we plant a garden, we prefer other kinds of trees, such as pomegranate and olive trees. This is because we want trees that bear fruit. We are the trees which God has planted in his garden. He is not concerned at how sturdy and beautiful we are, at how tall we grow, or at how smooth our skin is. As trees in his garden, he is concerned only that we bear fruit. And the fruit which he wants us to bear is spiritual: peace and love, faith and gentleness, patience and self-control, generosity and loyalty. Think again of the trees of the forest. From time to time we go and cut down one of those trees to provide wood for building and houses and fuel for our fires. If we do not bear fruit, God will cut us down and cast us on the fire. He has planted us on this earth not for our own sakes, but for his glory; and we can only glorify him by the spiritual fruits that grow in our souls.

54

Look at the world around you. It supplies all your bodily needs. It feasts your eyes with its beauty. And its glory reflects the glory of God, so it feasts your soul also. Look at the plants and the trees. Can you count all the different species? Can you describe all the different shapes of the leaves, the color and fragrances of the flowers? Look, too, at the animals and the insects. Are you not enthralled by their different sizes and shapes, by the different colors and textures of their skin and fur, by the different ways in which they move about and gather food? And then wonder why God has created all this. Has he created the marvelous universe just to supply our needs and to feast our eyes and souls? Or is there some other purpose in it all? The answer is that he has created all things—for their own sake. Each creature has its own purpose and destiny, which God in his infinite wisdom and love has planned. Do not try to understand God's plans; the human mind is hardly better than that of an ant in discerning the ways of God. Simply accept all his plans and rejoice in them.

55

Do you want to honor the body of Christ? Then do not despise his nakedness. You come to attend church services dressed in the finest silks which your wardrobe contains; and it is right that you should honor Christ in this way. But on your way, do you passed naked beggars in the streets? It is no good coming to the Lord's table in fine silks, unless you also give clothes to the naked beggar—because the body of that beggar is also the body of Christ. Do you want to honor the blood of Christ? Then do not ignore his thirst. You have donated beautiful gold chalices for the wine, which becomes a symbol of Christ's blood; and it is right that you should honor Christ in this way. But on your way to services, you passed by beggars who pleaded for food and drink. It is no good putting gold chalices on the Lord's table unless you give food and drink to the poor from your own tables. The service which we celebrate in church is a sham unless we put its symbolic meaning into practice outside its walls. Better that we do not come at all than we become hypocrites—whose selfishness can only besmirch the Gospel in the eyes of others.

Week by week you come to the Lord's table to receive bread and wine. What do these things mean to you? Do you regard them merely as some kind of spiritual medicine, which will purge your soul, like a laxative may purge your body? Or do you sometimes wonder what God is saying in these simple elements? Bread and wine represent the fruits of our labor, whereby we turn the things of nature into food and drink for our sustenance. So at the Lord's table we offer our labor to God, dedicating ourselves anew to his service. Then the bread and the wine are distributed equally to every member of the congregation; the poor receive the same amount as the rich. This means that God's material blessings belong equally to everyone, to be enjoyed according to each person's need. The whole ceremony is also a meal at which everyone has an equal place at the table. Thus we are celebrating our fellowship as brothers and sisters, with Christ as our unseen elder brother at one end of the table, and God as our unseen father presiding at the other end.

What does it mean to be as wise as a serpent? When a serpent is attacked, it is willing to have much of its body severed, as long as it saves its head. So to be as wise as a serpent means to be willing to lose everything—your wealth, your reputation, your friends—as long as you save your faith. Your faith is your head, by which you learn all truth; and by that truth your soul is set free. We should, however, recognize that the wisdom of the serpent is not enough; we must be as honest and innocent as doves. Indeed it is the combination of wisdom and innocence that creates virtue. The person who is wise as a serpent can sustain the most terrible attacks and still continue to flourish as a disciple of Christ. The person who is innocent refuses to retaliate against those who make the attacks. To be as innocent as a dove means never to take revenge on those who wrong you or undermine you. Unless wisdom is tempered by innocence, one attack provokes another, and conflict continues without end. Unless innocence is tempered by wisdom, a person is so vulnerable that he will not even survive a single attack. Rest assured that no one can ever take away your faith; your wisdom guards against that. But be careful never to bear a grudge against anyone who does you wrong.

When we see a person who has committed vicious sins and crimes escaping with impunity, we react with indignation. We want to see that person called to account and punished, and feel angry that this has not happened. But at such moments we should reflect on our own actions; indeed we should turn that sense of indignation inward against ourselves. Each of us should ask: "How many sins have I committed against others, when I have escaped with impunity?" There are, no doubt, many examples in all our cases. Recognizing this fact will cause our anger against others to melt away. More importantly, it will make us turn to God and ask forgiveness of these sins. Yet there is perhaps a difference between our own sins and the sins which we notice in others. Our own sins are probably quite subtle and inconspicuous, whereas the sins of others are obvious and gross. Should we, therefore, regard our own sins as less important or dire? On the contrary, we should realize that subtle sins are frequently the most harmful. Obvious sins, such as robbery and violence, are easily recognized, and so can often be guarded against by physical means. The more subtle sins, such as lying and slander and power-mongering, are frequently hard to spot, and so difficult to prevent.

Is it less grave to steal silver than gold, because silver is less valuable than gold? From the point of view of the victim, the loss of silver is less grave. But for the perpetration of the crime, there is no difference. To those who commit crimes, the sin lies in the attitude that causes the action, not the action itself. A person who can rob someone's silver will not balk at the opportunity of stealing their gold. If he does not steal for a period, it is probably because no opportunity arises or because he is ill. Thus if a person is to change his actions, his attitudes must change first. And a person will only change his attitudes if he realizes that his present attitudes bring misery to himself, as well as to others. Thus we must appeal to his self-interest, showing that by harming others he is cutting himself off from human fellowship; and revealing to him that his heart is hungry for fellowship, not for gold and silver. If we show that the way of righteousness is also the way of happiness than even the hardest of criminals will be eager to follow it.

Almost all of us at times find ourselves unable to sleep at night. We lie awake during the dark, silent hours. This rarely happens when our hearts and souls are at peace; it usually happens when we are troubled in some way. For this reason do not curse your lack of sleep. These times of wakefulness have been sent by God as a sign that something is wrong, and as a period for reflection. So when you cannot sleep, allow the thoughts that lie deepest in your heart to rise up to the surface. Often these thoughts are a reproach, telling you of a sin you have committed or an act of charity you failed to perform. If you have already confessed and made amends for these past failures, then you must assure yourself that God has forgiven you, so that you can sleep in peace. But if you have not confessed and made amends, then you must confess at once, admitting to God the precise nature of your sin, and asking forgiveness. Then you must plan how the following day you can put right your wrong. You might be so troubled that even then you cannot sleep. But do not worry: your mind and body will eventually sleep when your soul is at rest.

There are two types of sinners. First, there are those who are under an inner compulsion to sin: their hearts and minds have been so twisted and distorted, possibly through bitter experiences in the past, so that they can barely prevent themselves from sinning. This type of sin is really a spiritual disease; and we must try to heal such sinners with the same combination of compassion and determination which we apply to bodily diseases. Second, there are those who sin through moral indolence: they do not even try to resist temptation, but let their base desires and instincts rule the actions. Sinners of this second type can expect no leniency; it is within their power to stop sinning, so they must be punished if they continue. Think of the most extreme sin, that of murder. There are some murderers who, under certain circumstances, cannot help themselves; they simply lose control. They deserve our sympathy as much as their victims do; and while they should be prevented from repeating their actions, they should not be treated harshly. But the man who plans to murder someone for some evil motive—perhaps to steal his money—is entirely responsible for his actions; he deserves no sympathy, and must receive the severest sentence.

Let me describe to you five ways of repentance; each is different, but all point toward heaven. The first road is the acknowledgment of sins. If you acknowledge your sins to God, he will forgive you; and this act of acknowledgment will help you stop sinning. Let your conscience be your accuser, so that you will not have to face a far different accuser at the Lord's tribunal. The second road of repentance is the forgetting of the wrongs of others. This requires you to control your temper and to forgive the sins that others have committed against you. If you forgive others, the Lord will forgive you. The third road is prayer: not perfunctory routine prayer, but fervent, passionate prayer in which you lay yourself wholly before God. The fourth road is generosity, in which by acts of thoughtful love you make amends for the sins you have committed. And the fifth road is humility, whereby you regard yourself as having no virtue, but only sins to offer to God; he will then take the burden of sin from your back. At times it will be right to travel on one of these roads, at other times to travel on another. But ensure that every day you walk along at least one of them.

Are we all sinners because of the sin of Adam? Does the stain of sin pass from one generation to another? Does every man, woman, and child on this earth stand condemned by God unless they hear and believe in Jesus Christ? To most people this sounds utterly unreasonable and unjust; and indeed it is. To anyone who believes that God loves his creation, and especially loves humanity, it is inconceivable that he should condemn people through no fault of their own. The very idea that an innocent child deserves eternal punishment is monstrous. Yet it is utterly reasonable that we are made good through the goodness of Christ. Although the sin of one person cannot condemn humanity, the radiant love of one man can transform humanity—and is doing so. God waits for our hearts to open to his grace; he waits for an opportunity to reveal to each of us his truth. Then, when we are ready, he ensures that we hear about Christ and about his Gospel; and we find ourselves faced with a choice, which will affect the entire course of life and death—whether to embrace the words of Jesus Christ or to reject them. If we deliberately reject the Gospel, even when we fully understand it, then we condemn ourselves; if we embrace it, we shall ourselves be embraced by God in heaven.

Human beings are not consistent in the choices they make. One moment a person may choose to act in a most generous and self-sacrificing way; then a moment later the same person may act with greed and selfishness. Since God has given us freedom of will, he does nothing to prevent this inconstancy. Does this mean that human beings are actually incapable of following Christ? Will they constantly stray from the path of love which he reveals? The answer is both no and yes. We who regard ourselves as disciples of Christ are sadly aware of our own sinful tendencies. Indeed it is precisely because we know Christ, and can see his perfection, that we are so conscious of our imperfections; the comparison between ourselves and Christ is painful to behold. Thus we will always be inclined to stray from the path of love; day by day we will make wrong choices. Yet even to speak about "straying from the path" is to show that we can see the path and can discern the direction it leads. To be a disciple of Christ is not a guarantee of always remaining on the path; rather it is a commitment—a promise—to stay as near to the path as the will allows, and to struggle back onto the path after straying. This is as much as we can undertake in our own strength; through the grace of God we hope that over the years our journey will become straighter.

What does it mean to speak of Jesus Christ as God's Son? We may understand this in the earthly sense. When Jesus was on earth, teaching and healing the people, his will was in perfect unity with the will of God; thus we can speak of Jesus of Nazareth as the perfect embodiment of God—as God's Son. Similarly as our wills increasingly conform themselves to God's will, we can think of ourselves as the adopted sons and daughters of God. But we can penetrate more deeply than this into the mystery of Christ's sonship. Think of the sun. We do not make a distinction between the substance of the sun and its radiance; in fact, without its radiance the sun would not be the sun. Equally, we can make no distinction between God and the love which radiates from him; without that radiant love God would not be God. When we look upon Christ, we are looking at God's radiance; and the radiance is God. For this reason we cannot distinguish between God and Christ; and to express the unity between God and his love, we speak of Christ—the embodiment of love—as God's Son. It is a figure of speech; yet it is also literally true.

We sometimes try to distinguish between the divine and human aspects of Christ. We say that in the desert his divine nature restrained his appetites and desires, while his human nature felt hungry and weary. His divine nature healed people and performed numerous miracles; his human nature felt power go out of him at every miracle. His divine nature redeemed humanity on the cross; his human nature endured the most terrible agony. Yet is such a distinction between divinity and humanity valid? Can we actually see two quite distinct elements in the person of Christ? When we look at ourselves we can distinguish between the physical and spiritual aspects of our nature. We know that at times life becomes a battlefield as the spiritual and the physical aspects struggle for supremacy. Yet it would be wrong to say that the spiritual aspect should defeat and destroy the physical; rather we want harmony between the two. Our physical wants and desires should not be suppressed or ignored; rather they should be satisfied within the framework of morality which the spirit dictates. We should understand Christ in a similar way. It is not a question of his divine nature conquering and destroying his human nature; rather he revealed how human flesh and blood can live in perfect harmony with God.

Why did the devil attack Jesus, knowing that Jesus was without sin? The devil could not possibly have been victorious. Why did the devil, through Judas, hand Jesus over to be crucified? The death of Christ on the cross could not possibly have served the devil's purpose, except to give the devil pleasure in seeing Christ suffer. Nor could God have ordered the devil to attack and betray Jesus; the fulfillment of God's plan cannot belong to the devil, but must belong to God alone. In truth the whole matter worked the other way round. By attacking and betraying a person so manifestly good and holy as Christ, the devil exposed himself; the devil revealed himself as evil. This may sound strange; surely we know evil for what it is, without such a terrible exposure. On the contrary, the problem of evil is that it is usually disguised as goodness. Think of Judas. Throughout the early ministry of Jesus, Judas was a most loyal and passionate disciple. And he willingly went out with the others to proclaim the Gospel and heal the sick. Yet all the while, evil thoughts were seething in his heart; the lust for power and wealth burned within him. So when the opportunity arose to destroy Jesus, he seized it. Judas shows us how evil operates in the world; that is why God allowed evil to be exposed—by allowing Jesus to die on the cross.

Imagine a violent tyrant who afflicts the most terrible sufferings on all who fall into his power. People will hate him and be terrified of him; but many will acknowledge his right to mete out whatever punishments he wishes to those under his jurisdiction. Then a prince, the son of a king, comes into the tyrant's territory; the tyrant seizes the young man and executes him—although the young man had no evil intentions, but only good will. The tyrant is now exposed for what he is, because everyone agrees that his execution of the prince was unjust; and so the people rise against the tyrant to overthrow him. This is a precise analogy to the events surrounding Jesus Christ. The tyrant is the devil, and all those men of power and wealth who are motivated by the devil. These men afflict terrible suffering on the ordinary people of the world, impoverishing the people in order to satisfy their greed. But the people grudgingly acknowledge the authority of these men, and so do nothing to resist them. Then Jesus, the princely Son of the King of kings, enters their territory; they seize and execute him. In this way the men of wealth and power expose themselves for what they are. The question is whether the people will rise up against them, in Christ's name, and inaugurate God's rule of justice.

God has bestowed on every creature the gift of mutual love: every living creature naturally feels love and sympathy for its own kind. God has bestowed this gift most abundantly on human beings, whose capacity for mutual love is unfathomably deep. Indeed the love which Jesus expressed through his words and actions reveals the depth of love of which all people are capable. Thus our nature predisposes us to virtue. It follows, then, that vice is contrary to our very nature. When we are violent toward another person, we are violating our own nature. When we rob or exploit another person, we are robbing and exploiting ourselves. Vice turns nature itself into a battlefield. It sets the body against the soul. The body wants to do wrong in order to satisfy its lusts, whereas the soul wants to do right. Small wonder, then, that vice creates misery; a battlefield within a person's own nature can only destroy that person. The sign that you are being true to your nature is that the desires of your body are in harmony with the inclinations of your soul. And when your nature is at peace with itself, you shall be filled with joy.

Some say that marriage was ordained by God as a blessing to the human race. Others say that marriage is a necessary evil for those who cannot restrain their sexual appetites. In truth it is impossible to speak in such ways about marriage in general; we can only make judgments about particular marriages. There are some marriages which bring great blessings to the husband and the wife, to their children, and to all their neighbors. But there are other marriages which seem to bring few blessings to anyone. The difference between these two types of marriage lies in the spirit with which the bond was forged and is maintained. If a man and a woman marry to satisfy their sexual appetites, or to further the material aims of themselves or their families, then the union is unlikely to bring blessings. But if a man and a woman marry in order to be companions on the journey through earth to heaven, then their union will bring great joy to themselves and to others. Some people need a close companion, and for these people God has ordained marriage. Some do not need a close companion, and for these people God has ordained celibacy.

What shall we say about adultery? Let us ask an adulterer why he commits this sin. "It is the tyranny of lust," he replies. "Why," we ask, "are you under this tyranny? Why could you not satisfy your sexual desire through intercourse with your spouse?" The adulterer replies: "I am consumed with passion for someone else's spouse." Yet this very reply reveals the contradiction in which the adulterer places himself. If it is physical lust which impels him, then he could resist that lust; no physical desire is stronger than the power of the soul to resist it. If it is loving passion which impels him, then he should be repelled by the very thought of adultery: a truly loving man could not indulge his love for someone else's wife at the expense of his own wife. Besides, love can never force someone to do anything: love is gentle not violent, even when it is passionate. Sexual desire is a very powerful craving which even a life of celibacy does not suppress. But adultery is always a matter of choice; no amount of lust, and no passion of love, can overwhelm a person's capacity to choose between fidelity and betrayal.

When we speak of the wife obeying the husband, we normally think of obedience in military or political terms: the husband giving orders, and the wife obeying them. But while this type of obedience may be appropriate in the army, it is ridiculous in the intimate relationship of marriage. The obedient wife does not wait for orders. Rather, she tries to discern her husband's needs and feelings, and responds in love. When she sees her husband is weary, she encourages him to rest; when she sees him agitated, she soothes him; when he is ill, she nurses and comforts him; when he is happy and elated, she shares his joy. Yet such obedience should not be confined to the wife; the husband should be obedient in the same way. When she is weary, he should relieve her of her work; when she is sad, he should cherish her, holding her gently in his arms; when she is filled with good cheer, he should also share her good cheer. Thus a good marriage is not a matter of one partner obeying the other, but of both partners obeying each other.

A good marriage is like a spiritual castle. When husband and wife truly love and respect each other, no one can overcome them. If a man is unmarried and is attcked with lies and slander, his confidence and self-esteem may crumble; he may even begin to believe the lies said against him. But if he had a loving wife, she would reassure him with the truth, and so uphold his spirit. If a woman is single and is the subject of vicious gossip, she may feel that her reputation is being cut to shreds. But if she had a loving husband, his faith in her goodness and honesty would both comfort her and also impress those who doubted her. Similarly, a good marriage is like a buttress when a person's religious faith is shaken. Single people who are beset by religious doubts may feel that the house of God is collapsing around them, and that they are helpless to prevent it. But married people can turn to their spouse to express those doubts; and it is almost certain that the spouse's faith is sufficiently solid to allay those doubts. In the providence of God, when a husband is spiritually weak, his wife is spiritually strong; when a wife is weak, the husband is strong.

Those who treat their servants harshly, instilling fear into them with angry words and threats, may succeed in compelling their servants to work hard; but servants feel no attachment to such masters, and at the first opportunity run away. How much worse it is for a husband to use angry words and threats to his wife. Yet many men frequently try to intimidate their wives. They lift their voices and shout; they demand instant compliance to their every whim; they even raise their arms to force their wives to submit. Wives treated in this fashion become no more than sullen servants, acting as their husbands require out of cold fear. Is this the kind of union you want? Does it really satisfy you to have a wife who is petrified of you? Of course not. Indulging your ill-temper at the expense of your wife may give some immediate relief to your emotions; but it brings no lasting joy or pleasure. Yet if you treat your wife as a free woman, respecting her ideas and intuitions, and responding with warmth to her feelings and emotions, then your marriage shall be a limitless source of blessing to you.

75

When you are sick, you feel weak and feeble, and your face is pale; you are incapable of performing your normal tasks, and people remark how ill you appear. So you go to the doctor. What do you want from him? You say you want some medicine to cure your sickness. But if the cause of your sickness was cured, and you remained feeble and pale, would you be satisfied? Of course not. The truth is, a person goes to the doctor for relief of the symptoms of disease, not disease itself. The doctor, on the other hand, knows that the symptoms cannot be relieved unless their cause is overcome. Similarly, when we declare ourselves to be disciples of Christ, we claim that we want him to cure our spiritual and moral disease. Yet in truth we want him to relieve the symptoms, such as misery, discontent, despair, and so on. Jesus, by contrast, knows that he cannot relieve these symptoms unless he overcomes their deep, inner cause. And this is where the problems arise. While we would like to be rid of the symptoms, we stubbornly resist the efforts of Jesus to penetrate our souls. We do not want our deep-set feelings and attitudes to be changed. But only when we truly open our souls to the transforming grace of God will the symptoms of spiritual disease begin to disappear.

The sun gives forth light; it cannot help doing so. Animals breathe in and out; they cannot help doing so. Fish swim in rivers and the sea; they cannot help doing so. What, then, are the things which a Christian cannot help doing? First of all, a Christian cannot help praying. To be a Christian is to regard God as a loving Father; and it is natural to talk and listen to one's parents. Second, a Christian cannot help praising God and giving praise to him. To be a Christian is to affirm God as creator of the universe; and when a Christian looks at the beauty and glory of what God has made, praise and thanksgiving pour from the lips. Third, a Christian cannot help being generous. To be a Christian is to acknowledge that everything belongs to God, and that human beings are merely stewards of what they possess; so they naturally want to share their possessions with those in need. Fourth, a Christian cannot help reading the Scriptures and also studying the insights of other Christians. To be a Christian is to rejoice in the power of the Holy Spirit; and the Spirit speaks to us through the Scriptures and through the insights of our spiritual brothers and sisters.

Helping a person in need is good in itself. But the degree of goodness is hugely affected by the attitude with which it is done. If you show resentment because you are helping the person out of a reluctant sense of duty, then the person may receive your help, but may feel awkward and embarrassed. This is because he will feel beholden to you. If, on the other hand, you help the person in a spirit of joy, then the help will be received joyfully. The person will feel neither demeaned nor humiliated by your help, but rather will feel glad to have caused you pleasure by receiving your help. And joy is the appropriate attitude with which to help others, because acts of generosity are a source of blessing to the giver as well as the receiver. Indeed the receiver may only derive a material blessing, but the giver derives a spiritual blessing. If you give gladly, even if it is only a small thing, it will seem like a fortune. If you give resentfully, even if it is substantial, it will seem like a pittance.

We are taught to fast regularly as part of our Christian discipline. Why should we fast? How do we serve God by going hungry? Surely we need adequate food each day in order to work hard in God's service. Jesus criticized most vehemently those who drew attention to their fasting, urging us to fast in secret; so clearly fasting is not a matter for personal pride. There are two reasons to fast. The first is to break our attachment to material things, of which food is the most central, and so compel us to depend on spiritual things. When we are eating regularly, food not only sustains our bodies, but provides pleasure and satisfaction. In itself there is nothing wrong with such pleasure. But when we do without food, we are reminded that the only true and lasting source of joy is spiritual. The second is to express solidarity with those whose poverty forces them to go hungry. We may fast from time to time as a discipline; but many people fast continually because they have no money to buy food. If we are truly to show compassion to the poor, we must experience within our own bodies the consequences of poverty. Fasting is thus an incentive toward generosity. And the money saved during a fast can readily be given to relieve the enforced hunger of others.

We often speak of human emotions as having dimensions. One person is said to have deep feelings, while another is said to be shallow in their emotions. One person is said to have a wide and open heart, while another is said to have a heart which is narrow and closed. Of course, these are simple images; yet what do these images truly convey? When our emotions are deep toward a person or an event, it means that we cannot ignore that person or event, but must remain closely involved. When our emotions are wide and open, it means that we can respond to many people and events, not just a few. Jesus had deep emotions of love toward people, and he prayed deeply about every event in their lives; and he also had wide emotions, loving everyone he encountered with equal depth. This is how we must aspire to become. Shallow emotions lead to apathy and complaining; so they make us indifferent toward other people and toward the events which shape their lives. And narrow emotions enable us to ignore the cries of pain and suffering that we hear all around us. To be a Christian means to extend one's heart both downward and outward.

The world is full of problems. All of us have problems in our own lives. When faced with a problem, our initial reaction is usually to look at its outward symptoms, and to relieve them. For example, if a person feels his house is too small and the food he eats too rough, he will try to earn more money, and so buy a bigger house and better food. If one person is in conflict with another, they may both become angry, and each will try to defeat the other. Yet this is not Christ's way. According to Christ, the roots of all problems lie in the human soul; and that problem can only truly be resolved by transforming the soul. The man who is dissatisfied with his house and food will not become happy with more money; this is because one desire leads to another, so he will soon want an even bigger house and even better food. Happiness for him can only be achieved by looking inward, and learning to enjoy whatever life has; and this requires transforming greed into gratitude. Equally the person in conflict with another may look inward and learn to love his enemy; then the emotions behind the conflict will melt away, and reconciliation becomes possible.

There are many moments recorded in Scripture when the disciples were at a loss for words, or when their words were utterly inadequate. Faced with some wonderful revelation of God's glory, their tongues were tied. And since the description of these revelations in Scripture comes from these same disciples, we must sadly acknowledge that we can never know fully what occurred. Since each of us would have wanted nothing more than to have been witnesses of Christ's earthly ministry, we naturally feel deep regret at the lack. Yet God has deprived us for a purpose. He does not want us constantly to look back at those events hundreds of years ago. Those events are signs of what we should seek and discover here and now. Since Jesus healed people of their sicknesses, we should evoke that same miraculous power today. Since Jesus revealed himself in glory on the mountaintop, we should look for all the reflections of God's glory in the people around us. Since Jesus transformed people's souls, turned hatred into love and bitterness into sweetness, we should strive for that same transformation in our own lives. When God reveals his glory here and now, we, too, are at a loss for words; but in our dumbness we understand better the events described in Scripture.

I look at the city in which I live, and see only turmoil. I see men cheating one another, so that those who are most devious grow rich at the expense of those who are most honest. I see men being unfaithful to their wives, consorting with prostitutes rather than sleeping in their marriage bed. I see men planning all sorts of schemes to gain power, putting down all who oppose them. I see empty churches, because people know that the teaching goes against all they want to achieve. I see the clergy and bishops devoting their attention only to the material assets of the churches, while ignoring the sick and the dying, the poor and the needy. And I can hear no voices crying out against all this. What hope can we find in such a black and terrifying picture? Our hope must lie in the ultimate power of good over evil—and the knowledge that the power can work in even the hardest of men. If I stare long enough into the faces of the cheats and the adulterers, the power-mongers and the wealth-mongers, I can discern the faint traces of goodness and truth; I can find softness amid this hardness. While I can still see these traces, I will not despair.

The sea is surging and the waves are high: but we have nothing to fear because we stand on a rock—the rock of faith. Let the sea surge with all the power at its command, and let the waves rise as high as mountains; the rock on which we stand will remain firm and unshaken. Do I fear death? No, because on the rock of faith I know that death is the gateway to eternal life. Do I fear exile? No, because on the rock of faith I know that I am never alone; Christ is always beside me, my friend and my brother. Do I fear slander and lies? No, because on the rock of faith I know that I am always protected by the truth—Christ, who is the truth, is my protector. Do I fear poverty? No, because on the rock of faith God also provides for my needs. Do I fear ridicule? No, because however low I may sink in the esteem of those without faith, on the rock of faith all are treated with respect. Far from fearing the surge of the sea, I enjoy it, because it assures me that the rock on which I stand is immovable.

I shall soon be far away from those I love. I shall soon be cut off from the brothers and sisters whom God has given me. I shall be driven by evil men from the place where God has called me to live and work. I confess that I am sad. I may even say that I am bitter. I will add that I am angry. But I do not despair. On the contrary I feel hope. The source of my hope is the knowledge that, though I shall be separated from my brothers and sisters in body, I shall not be separated in spirit. The proof of this is in Christ. The first apostles knew him in body; and when he was crucified, they feared that they would be separated from him forever. But as he himself had prophesied, the bodily separation brought them even closer in spirit. After his death they knew him in the very depth of their hearts. Equally, when I am separated in body from my brothers and sisters, I shall know them even more deeply than I know them at present. In this knowledge my sadness will melt away, my bitter emotions will grow sweet again, and my anger will be soothed. Nothing can destroy love which is rooted and founded in Christ.

About the Author

Robert Van de Weyer is an Anglican priest and the founder of the modern-day spiritual center which is patterned after an earlier community established in 1626 at Little Gidding, near Cambridge, England, by Nicholas Ferrar. Like the earlier foundation, the community attracts both families and singles, who follow a simple rule and practice of prayer.

Among the many works that Robert Van de Weyer has compiled are *Daily Readings with Søren Kierkegaard; Daily Readings with Blaise Pascal; The HarperCollins Book of Prayers: A Treasury of Prayers Through the Ages; Feasts and Fasts: A Cycle of Readings for Advent, Christmas, Lent, Easter and Pentecost;* and *Revelations to the Shepherd of Hermas: A Book of Spiritual Visions.*

Also from Triumph™ Books

Triumph Christian Thinkers

These volumes provide stimulating and accessible introductions to the lives and works of the most influential Christian thinkers who will continue to shape our spiritual heritage into the next century. Each contains essential details of biography and thought, expert appraisal of the contribution of each, and is based on up-to-date scholarship. Included are the following: